Collins Primary Sc

OUR SENSES

Linda Howe

Resources Needed

Collections To Be Made

A collection of small objects (1)

Magazine pictures of food (4)

Fabric samples of different thicknesses (10)

General Resources

Box (1)

Wrapping paper (1)

A bag (1)

Scissors (1,4,10)

Pieces of cloth (1,6,10)

Yoghurt pots (2,11)

Greaseproof paper (2)

Rubber bands (2)

Paper (3,4,10)

Pencils (3,4)

Cassette player (3)

Glue (4,8,10,11,12)

Shoe bag (6)

Plastic bottle (6,14)

Sand (6)

Foil (6)

Drinking straws (8)

Card (8,9,12)

Coloured pens (8,12)

Dried pasta, peas, lentils, rice etc. (9,11)

Chalk (10)

Sewing machine (10)

Coloured acetate (12)

Wax crayons (12)

Glitter (12)

Small dishes (13)

Other Resources

Coffee (2)

Teabags (2)

Cocoa (2)

Marmite (2)

Talcum powder (2)

Flour (2)

Icing sugar (2)

Powdered milk (2)

Tape of recorded household sounds (3)

Alarm clock (6)

Scarf (7,9)

Walking stick (7)

Skipping rope (7)

Herbs, fresh and dried (13)

Spices (13)

Telescope and/or binoculars and/or camera (14)

Contents

	Resources needed	2
1	Hands can feel	4
2	Tasting and smelling	6
3	Sounds around us	8
4	Favourite smells and tastes	10
5	Whose voice?	12
6	What will sound travel through?	14
7	Can you guide a 'blind' friend?	16
8	Finding out about eyes	18
9	Braille signs	20
10	Feeling with gloves	22
11	Making shakers	24
12	Crazy sunglasses	26
13	Smelling plants	28
14	Looking through things	30
	Acknowledgements	32

1 HANDS CAN FEEL

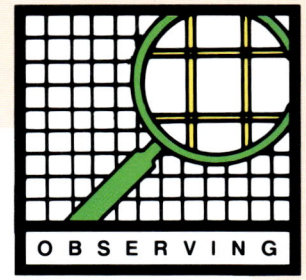

Look at your hands. Can you point to your:
- fingers?
- thumbs?
- palms?
- wrists?
- knuckles?
- nails?

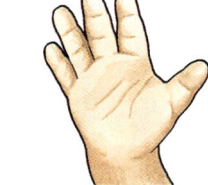

Draw a picture of your hands and label the parts.

Look again at your hands. Which parts do you feel with? What else can you do with your hands? Think of some things that you do with your hands indoors and some things that you do with your hands outdoors. Think of some more things that you would find very difficult to do without hands. How would you paint, write, ride a bicycle or eat your dinner?

What else could you not do?

Put your hands behind your back and try to put your feet in your shoes. Then try something like playing football. Think of some more things to try with your hands behind your back.

How much can our hands tell us?

YOU NEED: A collection of small objects   A box   Wrapping paper   A bag   Scissors   A piece of cloth

 Put all the objects in a bag so that nobody can see them. Sit in a circle. Ask one person to turn round and put their hands behind their back. Choose one of the objects and put it in their hands. Can they guess what they are holding?

Ask questions to help the holder find out about the object by feeling. You could ask if it's:
- long or round?
- warm or cold?
- hard or squashy?
- stretchy?
- bendy?
- rough or smooth?

What else could you ask them?
Is it fair to ask about colour?

Make a feely box.
Find some things to put in the box for a feeling game.

Write some clues for a mystery object. For example: I am cold, smooth and long with a rounded end. I will not bend. What am I?

2 TASTING AND SMELLING

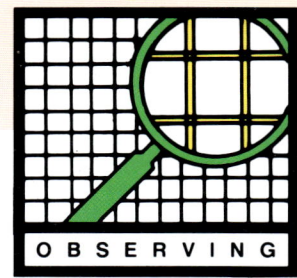

Think about your favourite smell. It could be the smell of something to eat, something cooking, new shoes, fresh clothes, cut grass or talcum powder.

Think of some other things which could be nice to smell. You could make up a poem about your favourite smells. First write down all the things you can think of and then try to put them together in a poem. You could draw some pictures to go with it.

Are some of the things which are nice to smell also nice to taste? Make lists of things which are:
- nice to smell but not to taste
- nice to smell and taste
- nice to taste but not to smell

Can you think of things which taste:
- salty? • sweet? • bitter?

Think of as many other taste words as possible.

Matching things by taste or smell

YOU NEED

16 Yoghurt pots or plastic cups
Greaseproof paper   Rubber bands   Coffee
Teabags   Cocoa   Marmite   Talcum powder
Flour   Icing sugar   Powdered milk

ACTIVITY -A-

Use eight plastic cups.
Make two cups of coffee, two cups of tea, two cups of cocoa and two cups of Marmite.
Mix them all up.
Can you find the pairs by smelling and tasting?
Are some easier to tell than others?

ACTIVITY -B-

Put talcum powder in two clean cups, flour in two more, icing sugar in the next two and powdered milk in the last two.
Put a piece of greaseproof paper over each one and fix it with a rubber band.
Make small holes in the greaseproof paper and mix up the cups.
Can you find the pairs by smelling?

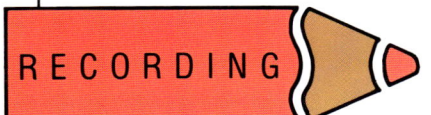
RECORDING

You could write words for smells and tastes and put them into a class book or individual books.

SOUNDS AROUND US

Sit quietly for one minute.
Write down or draw pictures of any sounds you have heard.
How many different sounds did you hear?
Try again at another time of day.
What do you hear now? How many sounds do you hear again?
How many sounds are new sounds?

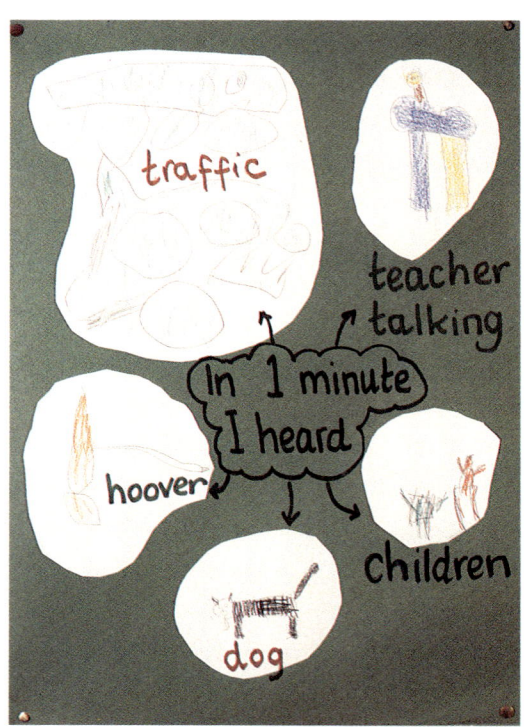

Can you think of some sounds that we might hear at any time of day?
What about sounds that we only hear sometimes?
Here are some ideas to help:
- dinner time sounds
- playtime sounds
- starting school sounds
- end of school sounds

Think of your own ideas.
How might these sounds be different from others? Which sounds do you think you hear most often?

Guess what made the sound

YOU NEED
Tape of recorded household sounds (such as door bell, vacuum cleaner, alarm clock, washing machine) Cassette player Paper Pencils

Listen to the tape. Write down or draw a picture of what you think made each of the sounds. Now listen again and find out what everyone else thought. Which sounds were easiest or most difficult to guess?

Use the cassette recorder to make a tape of sounds around the school. Can others guess what made them? Try to find some sounds that will be hard to guess.

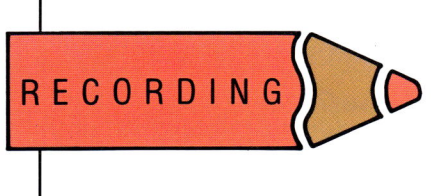

A chart will show at a glance which sounds were easiest and hardest to identify.

9

4 FAVOURITE SMELLS AND TASTES

Imagine that you have a magic sweet. It can taste of anything you want it to. Write a story about what you would make it taste of, or draw or paint a picture.

SOMETHING TO TRY

In cold weather you could put out some bird food. Put it out in piles of different kinds. You might try piles of:

bread   nuts   seeds   bacon rinds, cut small   fruit

What else could you put out?
Which pile goes first?
Which one is left until last?
Why do some go sooner than others?
Watch to see if some birds like one pile better than other piles.
Make lists of any birds that you see and their favourite foods.

Draw a picture of all your favourite foods.

What are your favourite foods?

YOU NEED   Paper   Pens and pencils   Glue   Scissors
Magazine pictures of food

 Find out everyone's favourite foods.
Ask everyone to write their name and either draw or write their favourite food on a piece of paper (one piece for each child).
Now use the pieces of paper to make some sets. You could try sets of:

- foods (chips, cake, jelly, etc.)
- savoury/salty, sweet/sour tastes
- foods from animals
- foods from plants
- foods from both animals and plants
- foods we eat at different meals

as well as your own ideas.

 Cut out some pictures of food. Draw some sets and stick the pictures on to make sets of savoury and sweet foods.

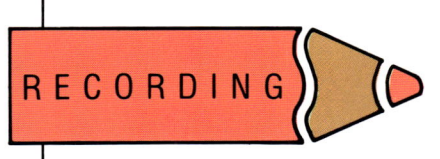 The sets themselves form the record.

5 WHOSE VOICE?

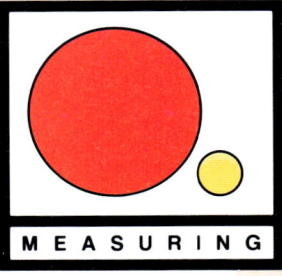
MEASURING

Hearing sounds from a distance

ACTIVITY -A-

Four children should stand in a row. Everyone else turns so that they are facing away from them.
One child says, "Hello".
Can the others say who spoke?
Try again and change over so that different children have turns. Are some voices easier to guess than others?

ACTIVITY -B-

Try again with different children, but this time they should only whisper. Is it easier to tell who is speaking if they speak normally or whisper? On a nice day you could go outside and try shouting. When is it easiest to tell whose voice it is – when they are speaking, shouting or whispering?

ACTIVITY -C-

Try the game again, but this time let two children speak together. Are some voices stronger than others?

ACTIVITY -D-

You need a big area like a playground or the school hall. Find out how far away you can go and still hear a sound. You could clap, sing, hum or, in a bigger area, use a bell, drum or anything else you can think of.
Send one child as far away from you as possible. Ask them to walk towards you making the sound.

Put your hand up when you hear it.
When everyone's hand is up, the child stops.
How close to you did they get?
Now try some other sounds.
Which sounds travel furthest?
Do they travel further than a speaking voice?

 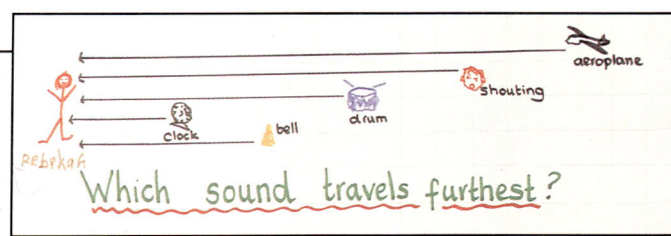

Make a chart like this to show which sounds travelled furthest.

6 WHAT WILL SOUND TRAVEL THROUGH?

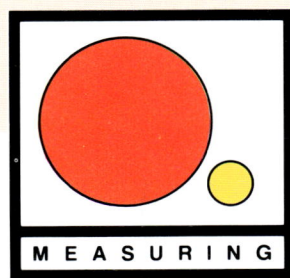

MEASURING

What noises do these animals make?

cats   dogs   horses
sheep   pigs   elephants   monkeys

Think of as many animals as you can and the sounds they make.
Some animals make more than one noise.
How do cats show that they are happy?
How do dogs show that they are fierce?
Think of some more animal noises that tell us what an animal is feeling.
Can you make some of the noises?
You could sing *Old Macdonald Had a Farm*.
You might add some new verses for *Old Macdonald Had a Zoo*.

Make a book of animal noises. Draw or find pictures of animals to stick in the book and write the noises round the pictures.

Can you find out what sound can travel through?

YOU NEED

Alarm clock   Different fillings   Shoe bag
Plastic bottle filled with water
Biscuit tin   Pieces of cloth

 Make the alarm clock ring.
Put it in the bag and let it ring again.
Put it in the tin and let it ring once more.
Where does it sound loudest? Where is it the quietest?
Why do you think this is?
Can you find a filling for the bag that will make the alarm clock quieter?
Can you find a filling that cuts out the sound completely?

Hold the clock to your ear.
Can you hear it tick?
Try holding the bottle of water to your ear and ask a friend to hold the clock the other side of the bottle.
Can you still hear the tick? Hold some cloth over your ear.
Can you hear the clock through it? What else can you hear it through?

Draw the clock and all the things that you can hear it through.

7 CAN YOU GUIDE A 'BLIND' FRIEND?

What do you think it is like to be blind? Close your eyes and think of some things that you could not do if you were blind.

How would you read?
Have you heard of a talking book? People read stories onto a tape which is sent to blind people. Talking newspapers are also made in this way. Perhaps you could read or tell a story on a tape. Play it back and listen to it with your eyes closed. Does the story come to life? Find out if your local library has talking books. They might like your tape for blind children.

What else can be used to help blind people? You might have seen people with a white stick. What does this tell us? You might have seen someone with a guide dog. The dog has to be very clever and obedient. Why do you think that guide dogs must be carefully trained?

Guiding a blindfolded friend

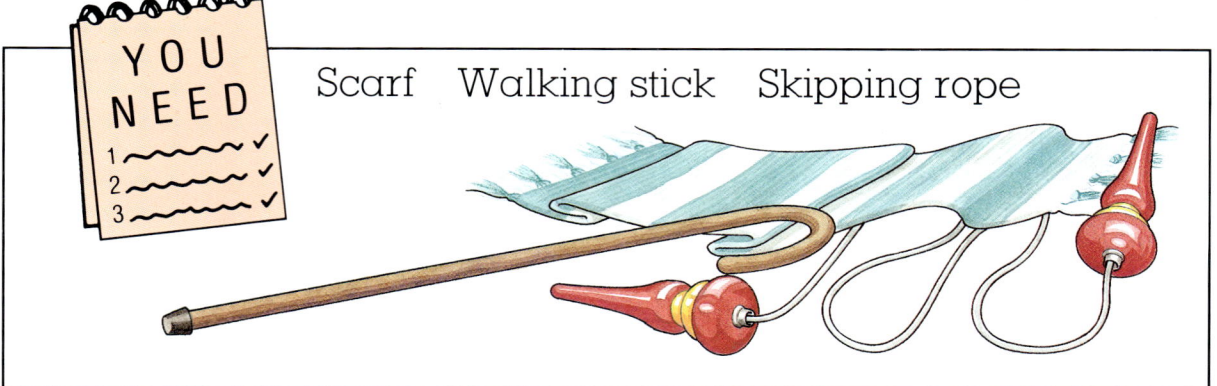

YOU NEED   Scarf   Walking stick   Skipping rope

Work in pairs. Ask your partner to put a blindfold on. Change the position of the furniture in the room. Tell your friend how to walk from one side of the room to the other.

You must say where to go and when to turn. How easy is it to guide someone?

Change over so that you now wear the blindfold. Your partner can change the furniture again. Try using a walking stick to help walk across the room without bumping into anything.

Put a skipping rope around a friend's waist. You should wear a blindfold. Can your friend guide you?

You could write down instructions for a friend so that they could get around the classroom without being able to see. You could also use the Logo program on the computer to move around the screen.

FINDING OUT ABOUT EYES

Have you ever had your eyes tested?
Did you have to look at a chart?
What did the chart have on it?
Did it show big and little things?
Make a chart to test someone's eyes. What will go on the chart?

Sometimes our eyes play tricks on us. Try these:

Which is the longest line?
Which is the shortest line?
Use a piece of string to
measure. What do you find
out?

Which vase has the widest
top? Measure and find out.

We call these optical illusions.
Can you make up some more
of your own?

Finding out about eyes

YOU NEED
Card circles (5cm to 10cm diameter)
Small, rigid drinking straws   Card
Coloured pens   Glue or sticky tape

 Take two card circles.
On one draw a large goldfish bowl.
Draw a small fish in the middle of the other.
Stick a drinking straw to the back of one circle and then stick the two circles together so that the pictures are outside.

Twist the drinking straw between your hands and watch what happens.
What do you see?
If you twist it carefully you should see the fish in the bowl.
Take two more circles. Can you think of other ideas?

You could try:

    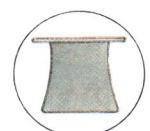     

a boat on a pond   a rabbit in a hat   a bird in a tree

 Test to find out which colours we remember best. Draw coloured spots on pieces of card. Show them to a friend for three seconds. Which colours do they remember first? Try it with other friends.

Make a chart with coloured spots. Do you see a pattern of colours?

BRAILLE SIGNS

A Frenchman called Louis Braille found a way to make writing which blind people can read by touching. The letters are made up of little bumps so that you can feel dots under your fingers. You might be able to find a Braille book to feel. It is not very easy to feel the dots as they are small and close together. Why do you think the dots have to be quite small?

SOMETHING TO TRY

Each Braille letter is made from a pattern of six dots which fit into a rectangle. Each letter has a different pattern of dots.

Draw six small squares in a rectangular pattern on a piece of paper. Using six counters, cubes or buttons find as many different ways as possible to cover some of the squares. Can you find a Braille alphabet to show you which letters you have made?

Can you make your name so that the letters can be felt?

YOU NEED: Card   Strong glue   A blindfold
A collection of textured items

Write your name on a piece of card. Make each letter fat so that you can stick something on it.
Choose things that will be easy to feel and stick them on to fill in the letters.
If you have a long name your initials will be enough.
Leave your name to dry.

Ask a friend to shut her eyes and put one of the name cards in front of her. Can she say whose names she is feeling?
Which names are easiest to feel? Which is the hardest?
Is this because of the texture used or the length of the name?

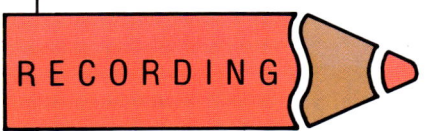

The name cards are a record in themselves. You could make two sets. One set could show those names that were easy to recognise by feeling and the other those that were difficult.

FEELING WITH GLOVES

Try using your hands very quickly.
Play some games with a sand timer.
- Who can put the most pegs on a line in one minute?
- Who can make the biggest or tallest Lego tower in three minutes?
- Who can spoon the most marbles into a pot in one minute?

For the last game you can stand a flower pot upside down in a big bowl and try and see how many marbles you can get through the hole in one minute.

Can you think of some more games to play which test how quick and careful you can be?

SOMETHING TO TRY

Take off your shoes and socks. Can you pick up something with your feet? You could try picking up a sock or a shoe with one foot. Is it easier with one foot than the other? Can you think of a game to find the quickest feet?

Making gloves to find out which material you can feel through

YOU NEED
Fabric samples of different thicknesses
Chalk   Glue   Scissors   Paper
Sewing machine (optional)

Draw round one of your hands on a piece of paper. You could make a mitten shape or a shape with fingers.

Draw another line outside the first one and cut round this line. Put the shape on one of the pieces of material and draw round it with chalk.

Cut out two hand shapes from the material. Sew or stick them together. Does the glove fit your hand? If it does, make one for your other hand. If not, try again until you have a pair that fits.

Try some of the games you played before with gloves on and again with gloves off. What do you notice?

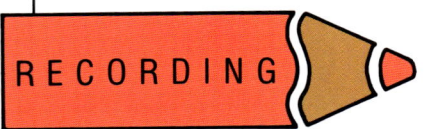

Record the scores on a chart like this to show how well you did with your gloves on and off.

Games	with gloves	without gloves
pegs on a line	6	11
lego blocks in a tower	4	15
marbles in plant pot	9	10
move the peas with a straw	8	7
drawing circles	12	20
cutting out squares	3	6

11 MAKING SHAKERS

Do you like singing?
What are your favourite songs?
Do you sometimes play an instrument?
You might play one which you bang or tap like:

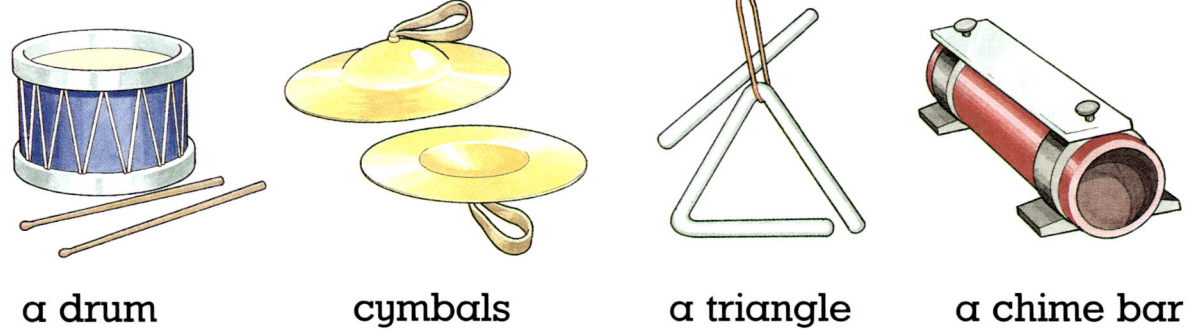

    a drum   cymbals   a triangle   a chime bar

Can you think of any others?

You might play an instrument which you shake, like:

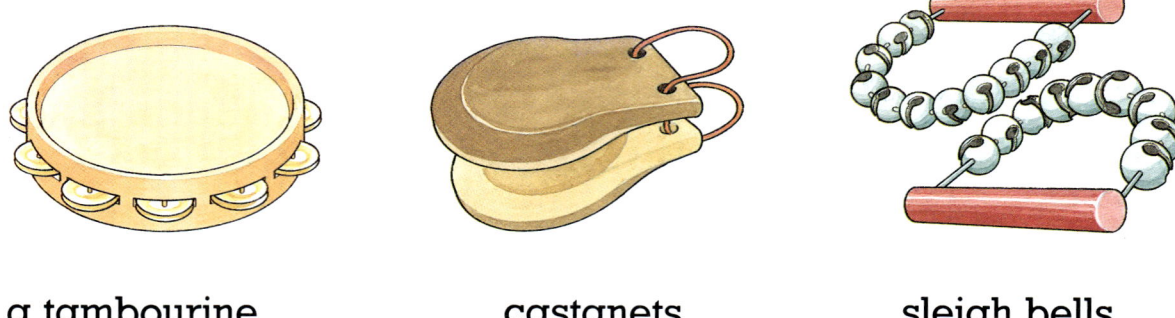

  a tambourine   castanets   sleigh bells

What else do you shake to make music?

Think of some more ways in which we make sounds.
Some sounds we can make with our bodies like:
clapping
stamping
clicking our fingers

Making a shaker

YOU NEED
Yoghurt pots   Strong glue
A variety of fillings

Decide what kind of sound you would like your shaker to make. It could be a loud sound, a soft sound, a rattle, swish or jingle.
What others sounds could you make?
Choose a filling that will make the sound you want.
Take two yoghurt pots.
Put the filling in one and stick the two pots together.
When the glue is set play your shaker.

What kind of noise does it make?
Can you think of ways of making the shaker better?
You might decorate it or add a handle. What else could you do?

Make sets of the fillings sorted by the kinds of sounds they make.

12 CRAZY SUNGLASSES

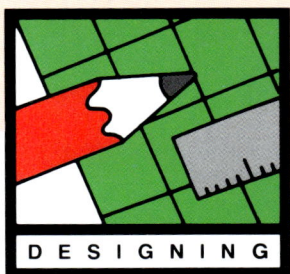

Why do some people wear glasses?
Do you ever wear glasses?
You might wear them to help you see clearly or to stop the sun from hurting your eyes. It is not safe to look at the sun.

Glasses are made of frames and lenses. The frames have pieces to go over the ears and a bit to sit on the nose. The frames can be all sorts of colours, shapes and sizes. You can see the frames in shops. The lenses are specially made for each person's eyes.

Making a pair of fun sunglasses

YOU NEED
Coloured acetate   Card   Wax crayons
Tape or glue   Felt pens   Glitter
Strips of thin card

Hold a piece of card over your eyes and get a friend to mark where your eyes are with a wax crayon.
Cut holes in the card where they are marked. Can you see through the holes? If not, make them bigger.
Now choose a shape for the frames. Do not worry about ear pieces. The shape could be:

   hearts   diamonds   stars   squares   triangles

You can also try an idea of your own.

Draw the shapes round the holes and cut round them. Make sure the glasses are joined together at the nose. Cut two pieces of coloured acetate. They could be the same colour or two different colours.
Stick the acetate behind the holes

Use a card strip to make a band to go round your head and join the glasses to the front of it. You can use felt pens and glitter to decorate the glasses.
Try them on. How do they change how things look?

 Write down how you made your glasses.

13 SMELLING PLANTS

INVESTIGATING

Can you collect some plants? You might go on a walk around the school grounds or in the park. Always ask permission before you collect any plants. When you have a collection, look at them carefully. Are they all the same
- colour?
- shape?
- size?

Can you see the different parts of each plant.
Can you see the:
- flowers?
- leaves?
- stems?
- roots?

Make a collection of leaves and draw all the different shapes. How many different shapes can you find? Do leaves of different plants have the same shape?

Smell the plants.
Do some have a stronger smell than others?
Which plant has the strongest smell?

Looking at herbs and spices

Herbs   Spices   A teaspoon   Hot water
Small dishes

Smell all the herbs and spices.
How many different smells are there?
Are there any things which smell similar?
Which smells do you like the best?
Crush some herbs in your hands.
Do they smell stronger now?

Mix different herbs in hot water. Does the water smell now?
Can you guess which herb is in the water just by its smell?
Can you make sets of strong and weak smelling herbs?

Choose two spices.
Put a teaspoon of each in a little dish and mix them. Is the smell of one stronger than the other, or does the mixture smell equally of both of them?
Try some other mixtures. Each time say which is the strongest smell. What else can you try?

Draw the fresh herbs in sets of smells (such as minty, curry, aniseed, etc.).
List the spices and ring the stronger ones.

14 LOOKING THROUGH THINGS

Making things bigger

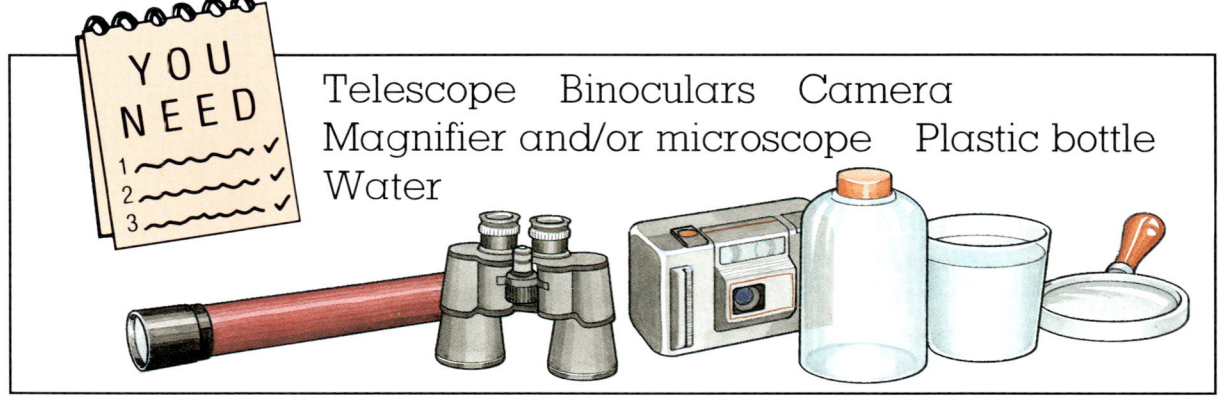

YOU NEED: Telescope Binoculars Camera Magnifier and/or microscope Plastic bottle Water

Find something small to look at. It might be:
- something far away
- a small object like a button

Look at the object carefully.
Look at it through a telescope, camera or binoculars.
What do you notice now?
Does the object seem bigger or smaller?
Does it seem closer?
Are there some things which you can see through the telescope, binoculars or camera which could not be seen before?

If you have a microscope you can look at things through it. How does it change what you see?

Write your name as small as you can.
Look at it through an empty plastic bottle. Do you see any changes? Fill the bottle with water, screw the top on tightly and look at your name through the water.

What do you notice? You can try looking at some other things through the water.

How does the water change what you see?
Look at someone who is looking at you through the water. What does their eye look like? Look around the classroom through the water. What looks different?

RECORDING

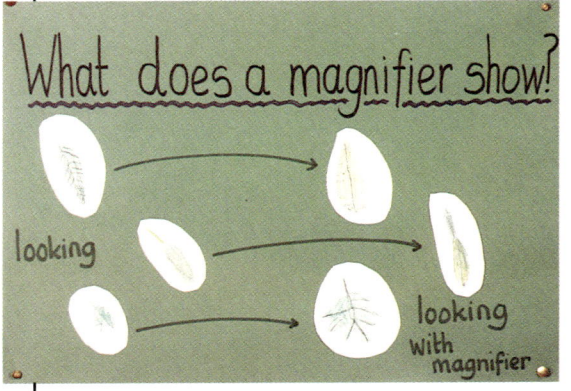

Fold a piece of paper in half. Make a line down the middle.
Choose a plant or a leaf and draw it on one side of the line.
Now get a magnifier and look at the plant or leaf through it. On the other side of the line draw what you see using the magnifier. Are there any differences between the drawings?

Acknowledgements

Copyright © 1990 Linda Howe
ISBN 0 00 317543 X

Published by Collins Educational London and Glasgow

Design by David Bennett Books Ltd.
Illustrations by Amelia Rosato and Sally Neave
Commissioned photography by Oliver Hatch
Picture Research by Nance Fyson and Gwenan Morgan

Typeset by Kalligraphics Ltd., Horley, Surrey
Printed and bound in Wing King Tong, Hong Kong

All rights reserved. No part of this book may be reproduced or transmitted in any form or by any means, without the prior permission of the publisher.

The publishers thank St. John's First and Middle School, Ealing, London and Woolpit County Primary School, Suffolk for their kind co-operation in the production of Collins Primary Science.